Self Talk

How to Train Your Brain to Turn Negative Thinking into Positive Thinking & Practice Self Love

ASTON SANDERSON

Subscribe to the Free Book Club at **www.walnutpub.com** for more books from author Aston Sanderson, and free new releases from Walnut Publishing.

CONTENTS

NOTE FROM THE AUTHOR

Dear Reader,

I hope you enjoy reading this book and that you find it helpful to you.

If you like this book, please leave me a review on Amazon. I personally read all my reviews and love to hear from readers.

You can leave a review by going straight to this page:
bit.ly/selftalkreview
Or you can find this book in your past orders on Amazon.

If you find any errors in this book or have suggestions for improvements, I would love to hear them. You can reach me at aston@walnutpub.com.

Sincerely,
Aston Sanderson

INTRODUCTION

Do you sometimes feel like your thoughts are racing, or you are your own worst critic? These feelings are quite common. Even if you don't feel this way, though, chances are: You talk to yourself. We all do.

Talking to yourself is what we refer to as "self talk." It is the ingrained patterns of thoughts that we run through our head, often unconsciously, day in and day out. It is the way we talk to ourselves *about* ourselves. For most of us, it's a habit we've probably never consciously thought about before.

In this book, we'll cover everything you need to know about self talk to use it to your advantage, instead of letting it control you unconsciously. Self talk has incredible impact on your self confidence, your progress toward your goals, your relationships, and even the way you live your life.

After you read this book, you'll have concrete strategies (and exercises at the end of each chapter) to make your self talk your own greatest ally in living your best life possible.

This quick-read will help you turn negative self talk into constructive, positive self talk.

CHAPTER ONE

What is Self Talk?

In this chapter, we'll discuss just what exactly "self talk" refers to, so we're all on the same page as we move forward in this book.

Self talk is your internal monologue. It is the thoughts that go through your head on a daily basis. Usually, it is how you talk to yourself about yourself. You may have never thought about your self talk before, or you may be aware of it. Either way, you'll learn a lot more in this book about harnessing your self talk for your own benefit.

The thing about self talk is that we all have it. While writing this book, I can't even count how many times I've talked to myself about it. I've said things like, "I didn't get enough writing done today," or "I should have started working earlier today." I'm sure you have a lot of similar thoughts when you are trying to complete a large project. Together, we'll learn how to better deal with these thoughts.

Our first step is to better understand self talk, so let's look at what it is.

SELF TALK IS OFTEN JUDGMENTAL

Is your self talk mainly negative, or mainly positive? There's also the option of neutral thoughts. You have probably heard of "negative self talk" and "positive self talk," but maybe not "neutral self talk."

Let's look at examples of all three:

Positive self talk:
- I am a good person
- My body is beautiful
- I killed it during my work presentation today

Negative self talk:
- I am not good enough
- I really need to lose 5 pounds
- I won't do well during my presentation tomorrow

Neutral self talk:
- I am a human
- I weigh 150 pounds
- I have spent 2 hours preparing for my presentation tomorrow

The neutral self talk examples probably feel a bit strange. They are simply facts, and two of them are quantifiable, meaning they are able to be measured by numbers.

When we talk to ourselves, we most often use judgmental self talk, whether we are judging ourselves positively or negatively. Our brain already knows facts, it doesn't need to state them "aloud" to itself. Our brain is meant for *processing* those facts. When we talk to ourselves, we are usually working through how we feel about something, whether that is our weight, our performance at work, or our general sense of self-worth.

Can you think of any things you've said to yourself about yourself recently?

In the next section, we'll look at how self talk shapes our lives.

SELF TALK IS THE STORY WE TELL OURSELVES

As a professional storyteller, I am especially invested in the power narratives hold over humans.

Storytelling is one of the most basic human needs, I believe. It is how we communicate with each other, how we pass down important culture, impart life lessons, and understand the world and our lives that are most often full of chaos, coincidence, and unpredictability.

We are all the main characters of our own stories. You are the leading woman (or man) of your life story. No matter the position you find yourself in today, you are probably creating stories to shape the past, your ideas about the future, and even your present self.

For example, maybe you tell yourself a story about graduating from a college with a bad reputation, so that is why you struggled to find your first job. Or maybe your story is that the college with a bad reputation forced you to work harder to prove your skills, so it was an asset to you, instead of a hindrance. Either way, the fact is the same about where you graduated from. It's just the story you shape around it to explain what it means to you and your life.

Maybe you have a story in your head about the future, like the best-selling mystery novel you will write. Maybe your story is daydreaming about going to the movie premiere from your book adaptation, and how glamorous it will be. Maybe your story is your friends and family laughing at you when they read your novel, thinking it is a piece of drivel. None of these things have happened, but they are all stories and judgments you are making up about the future, and they affect you right now, and the approach you take to writing that book (or putting it off forever).

In the present, self talk can feel kind of like a sports announcer, narrating our every move. In a soccer match or baseball game, however, the players can't hear the running commentary on their actions, so it doesn't affect them. But what if the players could *hear* the sportscaster saying, *"Ouch, what a bad pass that was,"* or *"He takes the plate with a low batting average this season. The odds are against him that he'll get this hit."* It would certainly change their performance! That's often how our own self talk can be — a constant (and not very friendly) announcement of our previous errors in a similar situation, recent mistakes we've made, how the odds are against us succeeding, and that our general stats are not good. To attempt to perform without hearing this constant chatter would be like being on the baseball diamond and needing to tune out a loudspeaker broadcasting your actions to thousands. Even though we're the only ones that can hear our self talk, tuning it out is not very easy.

No matter whether you are thinking about the past, future or present, you are creating stories by talking to yourself. These stories are not harmless; in fact, they shape your whole worldview and approach to life. The more you tell yourself the same stories over and over, the more true they become to you, whether they have basis in reality or not. And you may be entirely unaware of them! That's why in this book, I want to give you the tools to become aware of your self talk, and use it to help you shape the narrative about you and your life. With healthy self talk, you can reframe past events, understand yourself better in the present, and take action toward achieving what you want in the future. Harnessing your self talk can be supremely powerful, as you'll see.

Now that you better understand how self talk is the story we tell ourselves, before we get down to the nitty gritty of investigating and reshaping your own self talk, let's look at 7 types of negative self talk.

TYPES OF NEGATIVE SELF TALK

As we go through this book, we will learn to identify our negative self talk, how to investigate it, how to use more positive self talk in our lives, and other strategies for using our inner chatter to our advantage, to lead happier lives and achieve our goals. Our first task will be identifying negative self talk, so let's define 7 different kinds of *negative* self talk.

Filtering
Filtering can affect other types of self talk, and it is probably the most common form. The idea behind filtering is that when 10 good things happen to us, and one bad thing, we only remember the one bad thing. For example, if you received 10 compliments on a painting you created, but one insult, you'd probably only remember the insult, and you'd think about it a lot more, even though you got 10 times more compliments. Our brains are actually more inclined to remember negatives rather than positives due to evolution. It was helpful in caveman times, when you really needed to remember that a certain watering hole is where you almost got attacked by a lion, as it could save your life. Today, though, remembering and going over and over in our head the insults lobbed at us does little to help us lead better lives.

Example of Filtering: "Even though everyone said they loved my haircut, Jen said it was 'interesting.' Everyone else must be wrong, and only Jen is telling me the truth that my new haircut looks bad."

Catastrophizing

Do you ever find yourself going down a "thought spiral?" When one bad thing happens, does it suddenly remind you of all the things you are unhappy with in your life? This is catastrophizing. When one thing goes wrong, it seems everything goes wrong, or that one thing is blown way out of proportion.

Example of Catastrophizing: "I was late to work this morning. I probably looked disheveled when I walked in. Everyone probably thinks I'm a screw-up. I probably won't get that promotion now. And I have to go to the happy hour after work, and I'm always bad at socializing. And if it goes late, I'll be tired again tonight. I don't perform well when I'm tired, just like that huge history exam in high school that I bombed. I'll probably oversleep again tomorrow. I can't do anything right."

Personalizing

There is one main difference between optimists and pessimists. Optimists distance themselves from thinking about the negative things in life as a personal attack on them, and easily embrace what is positive in life. Pessimists tend to make excuses for reasons why the positive things that happen are flukes, and embrace worst-case scenarios as the norm and what they attract from the universe. Personalizing is making external events a reflection of you, even if they actually aren't. So when bad things happen, a pessimist, or someone who is using this tactic of negative thinking, will find a reason that they are to blame or caused it. It can be known as *internalizing*, and it also means taking external events a little too personally.

Example of Personalizing: "Jim said the party seemed 'quiet,' he probably meant that no one fun was there, even though I was. He thinks I'm not fun to hang out with."

Polarizing

In polarization, events or traits are seen as either 100% good or 100% bad. There is no in-between or gray area. Often, this kind of self talk goes hand-in-hand with perfectionism. If something isn't totally perfect, you may see it as a total waste. This kind of thinking is dangerous because even for largely negative events, there is often a silver lining. Even from largely positive events, there are still sometimes lessons to be learned for the future. Seeing the good and bad in most things is a more productive way to approach life and self talk.

Example of Polarizing: "I had one of my slowest runs this week, so my whole week of workouts was a wash. Why can't I get better and faster?"

Rehashing

Rehashing can also be known as *ruminating* or *dwelling*. Rehashing means thinking about the past, but in a negative, unproductive, and circular manner. Your thoughts may go over and over past events, leading you to wonder how things could have turned out differently if you had just won the game, not said the stupid thing, not gone to the party, not woken up late, not invested in that business, tried harder in school, etc., etc. and on and on. Often, rehashing can be associated with feelings of guilt or shame about things that have happened in the past that affect our self-esteem today.

Example of Rehashing: "If I just hadn't stayed late at the office that one night, my wife would have changed her mind about the divorce."

Rehearsing

Rehearsing is the opposite side of the coin of rehashing. Rehearsing is thinking about the future, but in a circular and unproductive fashion as well. This type of self talk often happens when we are nervous about an event in the future, or feel the future is too uncertain. We may be going over and over imagined conversations in our head, the different reactions we will get from people to our work we deliver, or imagining each step of our date. Preparing for the future has its place, for sure. But it becomes unhealthy when we become preoccupied with thinking about the future instead of focusing on the present, which is when we take action to prepare for the future.

Example of Rehearsing: "When everyone challenges my idea during the meeting, I'll make sure to bring up the failed team project from last year. I'll say…"

Blaming

The last of the 7 types of self talk is blaming. Blaming can easily fall into a negative self talk pattern that is hard to escape from. Blaming happens when we feel responsible for someone else's feelings of pain, or our own pain.

> *Example of Blaming: "Olivia wasn't having a good day, and I wasn't able to make her laugh. I'm a terrible friend."*

Now that you know a lot more about what self talk is, we'll look at why negative self talk is so harmful in the next chapter.

EXERCISE: WHICH TYPE OF SELF TALK DO YOU RECOGNIZE?

The exercise for this chapter is to choose which of the 7 types of negative self talk you identify with most. Is there one type that you know you use to talk yourself daily? Or most recently? This exercise will get you started in connecting your own self talk to what you read in this book.

CHAPTER TWO

Why is Negative Self Talk Bad?

Negative self talk can be hugely detrimental to us. It holds us back from achieving what we want, it keeps us feeling low, and it can just generally feel pretty crappy to have those thoughts racing through you head all the time. But there's good news, too. Turning your negative self talk around into positive self talk can mean that you have the self-confidence to achieve what you want, feel good about yourself, and feel happier without all those negative thoughts in your head.

In this chapter, we'll discuss in more detail the ways that self talk is harmful to us.

YOUR OWN WORST CRITIC

Self talk generally makes you feel down on yourself. Oftentimes, we are our own worst critics. Our friends and family would never be as cruel to us as we are to ourselves in our own head. Like it was mentioned in the last chapter, our brains are wired to focus on the negative. So when it comes to ourselves, we can feel there's a lot that we don't like. Maybe you feel down on your body or your weight, maybe you feel down on your skills or work performance, maybe you feel bad about your current or past relationships. The list can go on and on! Certainly, (and hopefully) we all have areas in which we have positive self talk as well. The importance is knowing in which areas we can be more susceptible to self criticism.

Saps Your Energy

Do you ever feel like your thoughts are racing when you feel something has not gone right, or you are feeling down on yourself? Often, having negative self talk in our head can be pretty draining for our mental energy. It takes a lot of effort to continually criticize ourselves day in and day out. Even if your negative self talk feels automatic and unconscious, it is still taking energy out of you.

That leaves less energy for making good decisions, assessing problems or situations accurately instead of skewed toward the negative, and using our brains for creative thinking, problem solving, work, or enjoying the moment. Feeling excessively worried or drained mentally is not something anyone enjoys.

Venting to Yourself

Sometimes people say that venting our frustrations can make them have less power of us, and venting is a healthy outlet for anger or annoyance. But for many people, venting only makes matters worse. Being annoyed by something is the first step, but then complaining about it is the second step to really cementing it in your brain. Venting can be helpful in some cases, but not many, especially not for small annoyances that we'd forget and move on if it weren't for talking about them all the time.

Can you think of that one super-negative relative you have? We all have someone in our lives like Uncle Steven who just won't stop complaining about "how awful the potato salad was at Aunt Mary's church barbecue last weekend, and how there were too many flies, why didn't she put out more fly traps? And auto repair shop Danny was there, and isn't he annoying, how many stories did he tell about his Yorkshire terrier digging up the garden, again?"

These may have been minor annoyances to Uncle Steve at the time, but now that he's been raving to anyone who will listen for weeks, they are causing him more distress now, even though the events are long in the past. He's making himself miserable, and some people seem to just love being miserable.

(Apologies to all actual Uncle Stevens who may be reading, by the way, I'm sure you're lovely people. If you're not, well, keep reading this book!)

Negative, internal self talk can follow the same pattern as venting out loud: It's almost as if you are venting about things, but to yourself. If something annoys you, and you say that to yourself in your head, it's effectively Uncle Steven sharing his story with everyone around him. Sure, you're not going on and on, but it's still creating a narrative in your head. When you go around and around in circular patterns, these things become routine, more memorable, and easily accessible.

SHOULD YOU TRUST YOUR BRAIN?

There is one last way that negative self talk can make you unhappy: If left unregulated, it can run wild, become routine, and get "stuck" in the same old patterns. Just like all humans get a bit "stuck" in our habits and ways of doing things, our thought patterns can get stuck, too.

Sometimes, we identify too closely with our thoughts. Remember that you are not your thoughts, and we will discuss this more in-depth in another chapter. If we trust that everything our brain tells us is true, we just believe any thought we can come up with. And as humans are extremely creative, we can come up with a lot of ways to negatively talk to ourselves and criticize ourselves.

But you shouldn't trust your brain, especially when it comes to negative self talk patterns you've been experiencing for years. Your brain may just be stuck. It takes more brain power, at first, to break these harmful patterns. But once you establish new patterns, the positive self talk patterns will be easier to maintain. Your brain is especially prone to tricking you when you are feeling emotionally bad. When you're in a bad mood, it's almost like you are wearing negative self talk glasses. Everything can seem to be going wrong. For example, if you're feeling in a low mood and it starts raining, you may groan and think about how rain is so depressing, how you forgot your umbrella, and how the rest of the day is ruined. However, if you're in a good mood, it's easier to see things through a positive lens. If it rains, you may feel happy thinking about all the flowers that will now bloom, or appreciate how the sound of rainfall is extremely peaceful.

Noticing our negative self talk when it's happening, and noticing our emotional state, will be helpful to changing those patterns as we go through this process together.

In the next chapter, we will address the myriad benefits to be gained by changing your self talk patterns.

Exercise: Your Inner Critic's Favorite Topic

The exercise for this chapter is to determine what area of your life your inner critic loves to chat about most through negative self talk. Is it your work? A specific past event? A relationship? Your body? Try to figure out which area your inner critic tackles the most with self talk, so you can move forward reading this book with an idea of what area you'd like to silence your inner critic in. Do not feel pressure to nail it down now, however. You can keep reading and learn more first.

CHAPTER THREE

Benefits of Changing Self Talk

In this chapter, we'll briefly discuss a few ways that changing your self talk from a negative state to more positive patterns will help you in your life. There really are so many benefits you'll see in every area of your life. It can help you feel happier, sleep more soundly, worry less, improve your relationships, improve your work, and help you in any area you feel you are struggling.

MORE RESILIENT

Resiliency is the ability to adapt to change and recover or work through bad experiences or setbacks. By learning more about the unconscious language your brain is constantly running, and gaining more control over it, you will better understand your reactions to things, your habits and yourself. When you are able to gain that distance from your own thought patterns, you are able to more accurately judge external circumstances. For example, if you aren't aware of your negative self talk, and your loan for a home gets denied, you may spiral into worry, stress, and low self-esteem, blaming yourself for the situation. However, if you are aware of your self talk and notice you are starting to blame yourself and throw a pity party, you can take a step back, recognize your reaction, and turn it into more positive self talk. You can recognize that this situation is not ideal, but think to yourself that you are resourceful, you have a big network, and you can figure out what steps you need to take to re-apply for the loan and get it approved and make a plan.

When you have more positive self talk, you don't get stuck in the trap of reacting to external events very emotionally. Your mental state will be stronger when bad times come, as they are sure to do at some point in all of our lives.

More Time for Creativity and Enjoyment

When you let go of a lot of negative self talk, you free up a lot of mental energy that you can put towards your work, being more creative, and enjoying the present moment instead of worrying about the future or rehashing the past. As mentioned in the last chapter, the inner chatter of our self criticism can take up a lot of space in our brain and use up a lot of our brain power. When you can stop those harmful patterns and circular thinking, you will have more time for creative thinking, or just relaxed, restful enjoyment of the moment.

Become a Better Leader

Negative self talk can lead to negative self esteem. When we feel badly about ourselves, it comes across in our body language, our actions, and our conversations. Have you ever heard the phrase, "confidence is sexy?" When people are confident, you can just tell. When they are nervous, it is also easy to see.

If you have more positive self talk going on in your mind, your actions, the way you carry yourself, the way you talk, it will all start to follow this more positive thought pattern you have running in the back of your mind. If you are in any kind of leadership position, it will make you a better leader, as people want to follow someone who is confident.

Self doubt affects your actions, and if you don't appear confident, others will question you more, too. This is especially important in leadership roles, but really, in any area of life, no matter your position. With enough work with your self talk, you will inspire yourself more, and eventually, others.

Achieve Your Goals

You may find that retraining your thought patterns also affects your behavior. As your self talk becomes more positive, your actions will become more positive, too. That's the idea behind the psychology of Cognitive Behavioral Therapy, which believes that thoughts influence feelings, and feelings influence actions. That's a very broad topic for another time, so for now we'll leave it at an example:

Talking negatively to yourself might lead to feeling badly about yourself, and then eating a whole pan of brownies to make yourself feel better emotionally, which then leads to beating yourself up about the brownies, etc. etc. But if you stop the negative thoughts before eating the brownies, and just think, "I feel down about myself right now, but this is just a low point, and I know I will feel better later," instead of thought spiraling, you can clearly *see* your thought pattern. Thinking "I am enough," even if you don't feel perfect all the time, can be enough to stop harmful actions that will make you feel even worse.

Did you know that athletes use purposeful and intentional self talk as a training strategy? When athletes don't harness self talk in their mind properly, their thoughts can naturally bend toward the negative and the critical. Many coaches have a mental training regimen for their athletes as well as a physical one, and it includes how athletes talk to themselves during training, before a big race or match, during their athletic event, and after. Positive and realistic self talk can be used to win Olympic medals, as it puts athletes in the right frame of mind to achieve what they want, and perform to the best of their ability when it matters most.

It is the same way in our own lives, for anything we want to achieve. Want to get a promotion at work? Want to write a novel? Want to start a business? No matter what your goals are, you can look at achieving them the same way that athletes do their goals. By using self talk as a motivational tool, you can become more productive and achieve what you actually want to in life. Achieving the goals we feel most passionate about is one of the hardest things to do. And making our dreams come true begins with our inner mental chatter.

Inner Peace

Sometimes, the insides of our minds feel like a battlefield. Our thoughts are like shots fired in a war between our rational selves, our optimistic selves, and our negative selves. Having all that back and forth is tiring, unproductive and stressful.

When you have more positive self talk, or are able to just gain distance from your negative self talk, you can feel more at peace with yourself. Your brain may be quieter or at least more friendly in its incessant chatter. When you recognize all these different thoughts and where they come from, you can pacify the different warring sides of yourself. Achieve more feelings of inner peace by going through the methods in this book.

Changing External Circumstances

Before we move on to the next chapter, there is one more important thing to note about the benefits of self talk. Often, we think we need to improve our lives by changing our external circumstances. We just need a new job, to lost 5 pounds, to find a boyfriend or girlfriend, or to buy a material object like the newest iPhone or gadget.

But changing your exterior circumstances will not change your tendency toward the negative when you have negative self talk patterns ingrained in your brain.

You may have negative thoughts about your body like "I am so fat. I don't like the way I look."

In our heads, we imagine that when we get skinny, we will magically have positive thought patterns. We imagine we will start looking in the mirror and saying, "Wow, I am so skinny and beautiful!" But even if you change your body, your negative thought patterns will remain the same. Once you have lost the 10 pounds you aim to lose, then you will look in the mirror and see new flaws to criticize, as that is the way your brain has been used to thinking. You may think, "I could lose more fat on my stomach," or "Why can't I build muscle in my arms? They still look flabby." Or, "I have no butt." And on and on. A pattern of negative thinking will stay a pattern. Our minds our quite creative; we can always find something to criticize. We will find more and more things for our negative mind to spin around in endless circles, and there will always be one more thing we need to change, no matter what.

However, if you change your ways of thinking, then you can set realistic goals, achieve them, and feel happy with your results. So, maybe health is something you'd like to change. You can still feel that you want to change your weight, as long as you know your brain will not magically change from unhappy to happy once you achieve it. In fact, with more positive and realistic thought patterns, instead of excessively negative ones, you will probably have an easier time achieving your goals of weight loss than with self-hating, self-defeating thoughts.

Are you ready to start moving forward with retraining your inner chatter? In the next chapter, we'll delve into how we will go about changing your self talk.

Exercise: See the Difference Between Your Negative Self Talk

and Imagined Positive Self Talk

Think of a goal you have that you have negative thoughts around. Maybe it is the example in the last section of this chapter, of wanting to lose weight because you feel bad about the way you look. Maybe it is a personal project you'd like to work on, but you feel bad about your ability to create it, like a novel, starting a website, or just writing a letter to a friend you've been putting off. Write down one or more negative thoughts you have about it right now, and why you feel unhappy about it.

Now imagine that you achieve that thing. Write down all the feelings and thoughts you imagine you'll have once you get it done. Can you see the difference in the negativity and positivity? Just noticing that you have these self talk narratives is the point of this exercise.

CHAPTER FOUR

How We Will Change Your Self Talk

In this chapter, we will outline the right mindset you need going into the task of changing your self talk.

When we were growing up, we had teachers, our parents, and other guardians looking out for us. As we learned about the world, we learned what actions were inappropriate, like knocking over our sister's block tower or throwing food, and which were appropriate, like sharing with others or talking in an "inside"-level voice. Our initial reactions and habits were corrected by the people around us. Now, you have to take control and correct yourself. You developed bad habits as a child. And they were corrected and set on a new course. So you can set your current habits on a new course, you'll just have to take the responsibility to recognize the person you are right now and the person you want to become. When we have fallen into negative self talk, the only way for us to notice and correct it is to be responsible for ourselves. If you are ready to take responsibility for your thoughts and actions, keep reading.

FIXED MINDSET VS. GROWTH MINDSET

I discussed this first principle in my book on Small Talk, but it is important for self talk, too.

The idea is the fixed mindset vs. the growth mindset. A fixed mindset means that you believe that who you are today is basically who you have always been and who you will always be. When someone has a growth mindset, they acknowledge that they are constantly changing. So someone with a fixed mindset would have self talk that sounds something like, "I can't run this 5k because I am not a runner." A person with a growth mindset would say, "I can run this 5k because I can train." Another example would be, "I can't learn French because I'm bad with languages" as a fixed mindset. The growth mindset would be, "If I put in the effort, I have the capability to learn French, even if it is a skill I find difficult."

Do you see the differences?

As you start to change your self talk, you will need to have the attitude that you possess the capability to change it.

From here forward, you can operate with a mindset of, "I can adapt my thoughts into new patterns, even if it is difficult," instead of, "Changing my thoughts is too hard. This is just how I think and how I am, and how I will always be."

STARTING SMALL: HABIT BUILDING

Changing your thoughts will be difficult. Up until now, you've probably not considered your self talk patterns. So being able to be aware of them, and eventually change them, will be a slow-moving process. But you should not give up if it feels hard at first.

Like building any habit, the original patterns feel quite rigid and stuck. It's like eating fast food every night for dinner and trying to go straight to chicken and vegetables. Changing all at once won't last, and won't be pleasant. But if you slowly start to change your habits, just one day a week, or one food choice at a time, it is easier.

So you will need to break up changing your self talk into smaller habits. A helpful metaphor when we think about changing our thought patterns is imagining that your brain is a forest, and the thought patterns you have are paths you've created over the years. It is easy to walk these paths: The trees are cleared, there are no branches in your way, and it is easy to see each step in front of you. As you try to form a new thought pattern, it is like going off the beaten path and trying to forge a new way. You have to hack at the branches and trees, and progress will be slow, instead of being able to race down the path you already have established. You also don't know the way forward. Which way should you make the path? But once you clear that new path, and walk it over and over, it will become as simple and ingrained as the first one.

It's also just like training your muscles: At first, you can't lift very heavy weights. But as you practice with those weights, then you can move on to heavier and heavier ones, and now your muscles are more defined, and you are stronger. Your brain is a muscle, and at first, you need to start with light weights. Be patient with yourself, and recognize where you are when you begin.

EASILY INFLUENCED

You have to believe that you can change. And you *can* change. Our brains and inner chatter, while they can be hard-wired over years and years of repetitive modes of thinking, are also easily influenced.

Have you ever been in the middle of a good book, and after getting lost in the chapters for a few days, you start to think in the pattern of the writing style of the book? Or if you've spent too much of your day on Facebook, you start thinking about life in Facebook statuses? Or if you spent all day looking at spreadsheets, then you have dreams about spreadsheets?

The outside world can heavily influence our inner chatter and thought patterns. All you need to do is make an active effort to contribute to that influence.

YOUR SELF TALK IS YOURS ALONE

One of the best things about changing your inner self talk is that it gets to be your secret. No one needs to know but you about the tactics you use for self talk, as most of them will be hidden inside your brain. Pretty wonderful, yeah? You get to choose how you talk to yourself.

As we move to the next chapter, in which we will begin describing the strategies and steps to change self talk, you may find that some strategies resonate with you and come naturally, while others don't. What's important is that whichever ones work for you, you work on. You may surprised which ones help the most. Try not to judge the strategies before giving them a try. No one has to know you are working on your self talk, it can be your little secret.

You are the boss here. If you are religious and feel most comfortable with religious thoughts that calm you, then go for that. If you enjoy getting woo woo about the universe or mother nature, do that. It's whatever you want. You have my permission to be as silly or as serious as you want.

We have outlined basic strategies to help you find general principles for talking to yourself, but there are a lot of blanks left open based on your particular situation. We'll guide you on HOW to fill them in, but you get to decide the WHAT.

In the next chapter, you'll learn the first step of changing your self talk: awareness.

EXERCISE: HELPFUL HABIT BUILDING REMINDERS

Rerouting your thoughts will be a slow process, just like building any habit. At first, it may be hard to remember to step outside of your thoughts and assess them. For this exercise, either use post-it notes or set up reminders on your phone to help you check in with yourself on a daily basis. You can put the post-it notes somewhere around your house where you are likely to see them, like your bathroom mirror, your computer monitor, the visor of your car, wherever you will see the reminder each day. Or, set up reminders on your phone to ping you several times per day to practice your new, positive self talk habit.

CHAPTER FIVE

The First Step is Awareness

The first step to remaking your self talk is to be aware of it. This sounds simple, but can actually be quite difficult when we're lost in a storm of self-criticism, self-doubt, and other negative tendencies that we're so used to we can't even see them.

Like we discussed in the last chapter, building a habit is slow-moving and takes effort. If you didn't do the activity in the last chapter of setting reminders on your phone or setting up post-it notes around your house, you may want to do it now to help you identify self talk.

MAKE THE MONSTERS LESS SCARY

Once you can recognize negative self talk, it's like shining a flashlight on a monster creeping around your bedroom in the dark. When you can see it, you realize it's not that scary. Now it has a name, and a shape, and once we see it, we can shoo it out of our bedroom with a broom. We'll get to the "broom" strategies in further chapters, but for now, let's focus on finding our flashlight and using it on that negative self talk.

Once you are able to identify your thoughts, you also gain some distance and perspective on them. Just getting a smidgen of distance from your negative thoughts, even if it doesn't feel like a lot, can make a big difference. Having the room to breathe from overwhelming thoughts makes them less powerful. You may begin to feel relief from your unending negative chatter even just by recognizing the thoughts.

What does recognizing and being aware mean?

When you identify a negative thought, you can label it. We will talk more about naming in a future chapter, but for now, you can use these phrases, or something similar, if you find them helpful:
- I recognize that this is a moment of negativity
- This is stress
- This is uncertainty
- This hurts
- This is a negative thought
- Ouch!

REMEMBER YOUR MOOD

It has been discussed how your mood affects your self-talk, but this is worth repeating again. When you are feeling low, you will be more susceptible to believing your negative self talk and following it wherever it wants to take you. When you are in an upbeat, sunny mood, it will be easier to dismiss negative self talk and think positively.

So awareness also means awareness of mood. Recognize what mood you are in and how that may be affecting your thinking.

CHANGE COMES NEXT

Once you have learned to become aware of your negative self talk, the next step will be changing those thoughts. But you can't change them if you can't first find them, so don't rush unless you feel comfortable first identifying your thoughts. Then we will begin the process of change. In the next chapter, we will learn about establishing some distance from your self talk once you have identified it.

EXERCISE

For this chapter about being aware of your negative self talk, you should try to write down a few self talk phrases you use as you notice them throughout the day. Try to write them down verbatim, nailing the exact language and phrasing you use with yourself. It can be anything you notice you say to yourself, and this exercise can be difficult at first, as these thoughts are so ingrained.

CHAPTER SIX

You are Not Your Thoughts

In this chapter, we will learn how to get some distance from our thoughts, and you will realize that you are not your thoughts, even though this may sound scary.

GETTING DISTANCE FROM YOUR THOUGHTS

Thinking about thinking is called metacognition. This is a common tactic in philosophy, but it may sound scary if you haven't heard of it before. Basically, in metacognition, you are able to think about your own methods of thinking. You could say that this whole book about your inner monologue, or conversation with yourself, or self talk, is about metacognition.

When you practice metacognition, you realize that you are not your thoughts. If you are able to take a step back from them, you can see that they just pass through your brain and can either get stuck, or you forget them and they continue moving on. A common practice in meditation is to view thoughts as cars passing by. You may be tempted to chase after good thoughts and stop bad ones, but practicing metacognition means just watching them going by, and trying not to judge them. Eventually, we will get to retraining your thought patterns for better thoughts, but for now, just realizing that you are not your thoughts is enough. It may be difficult to get a grasp on, but just spend some time thinking about this, however redundant that may sound.

One way to realize that your thoughts are outside of you is to say them out loud, and label them as thoughts. If you are feeling a bit overwhelmed by the amount of work you have to do, you may think: "This is too much, and I don't know how I'll get everything finished." But you can distance yourself from this thought by thinking, "I'm having a thought that this work is too much and won't get finished."

Even though identifying it as a thought or feeling seems like a small difference, it makes a big difference.

Where Does Self Talk Come From?

Where do the thoughts in our self talk patterns come from?

Are you the source of your negative self talk? Did you come up with this stuff, or did someone else? Investigate your negative self talk thoughts and think about where you first heard them. Were you influenced by pop culture or a TV show? Or someone in your family? The bully in middle school? Your mom? Figure out where they come from. Knowing the source helps to question their validity. Sometimes others criticize us for what they don't like about themselves; they put their insecurities onto us. Don't take on the cruel insecurities of others.

Your thoughts could also come from your limiting beliefs. You may need to look at the root cause, deep down of your negative self talk. Maybe your negative self talk is that you are lazy because you don't go the gym at least four times per week. You are telling yourself you are lazy, but what is the limiting belief deep down that keeps you in this negative loop? Maybe the belief is that you don't deserve to take some time for yourself, to better your health. And you believe this because the last relationship you were in, your partner didn't like it when you did things without him or her. So you feel guilty taking time for yourself. So your negative self talk comes from a different place, from your feelings about how much time you deserve for yourself.

You may find that some of your internal self talk is not true or accurate, but just something someone else has said or that you got from somewhere else. Remember, this chapter is about the fact that you are not your thoughts. Even if your thoughts tell you that you are your thoughts, they are wrong! Don't believe them! You can assess your thoughts to determine if they hold water or not. If they don't, you can change them, and in the next chapter we will look at ways to investigate whether a negative thought is true or not.

EXERCISE

For the exercise for this chapter, choose a self talk phrase you wrote down in last chapter's exercise, and see if you can figure out where it originated from. Do you know how long you have been telling yourself this thought? Do you remember where you first heard it? Does it come from someone else, or from a deeper belief you hold about yourself or your approach to life?

CHAPTER SEVEN

Questioning a Negative Thought

In this chapter we will look at how to "interrogate" a negative thought, as if you have sat it down in a single-bulb interrogation room and are getting ready to find out the truth from this pesky negative self talk. First, we'll look at "parking" your thoughts, and then we'll get to the questions you can use to analyze them.

"Parking" a Thought

The first step in interrogating your negative self talk thought is to get it into the interrogation room. Earlier, we spoke about the metaphor of your mind being a crowded street. The thoughts are cars racing by, and some of them are good, some of them bad. So to interrogate a thought, we first have to "pull it over," or "park" it.

What that means is simple: You just become aware enough of the thought, maybe even writing it down, to stop it in its tracks for some assessment. As discussed in the previous chapters, that isn't always easy, but that doesn't mean it can't be done. All you need is a little practice to become familiar with recognizing your negative thoughts to park them.

So, once you've effectively parked a thought, the next step is the interrogation. We will look at some questions you can ask your thought to assess its validity.

Interrogating a Thought

OK, let's get down to the good stuff: Let's see just how true that negative self talk thought you're having is.

Once you identify a negative thought you are having about a situation or yourself, you can break it down and deconstruct it.

Ask yourself:

- Who is this important to?
- How much does this matter in the long run?
- Is my response an overreaction?
- Am I overgeneralizing?
- What is the concrete evidence for this thought?
- Am I viewing things in terms of absolutes? (Remember the "polarizing" type of negative self talk from the first chapter.)
- Should it be more of a gray area?
- Am I assuming the thoughts or feelings of others?
- Am I using cruel language?
- If I were having a positive thought about this, how would I interpret things?
- What is the worst thing that could result from this? How likely is that to actually happen? If it did happen, what would be the next step I would take?
- Could the situation or feeling be worse?
- Is this thinking going to help me achieve my goals?
- What would help me feel better or think a different way?
- What can I learn from this thought?
- What is another way to interpret the situation? What would that mean?
- What physical evidence for this exists, and how much is my feeling or perception?
- What is the evidence for my conclusion?
- How would a friend talk to me about this thought?
- How would someone from a different culture or upbringing feel about this thought?
- If I am ruminating on a choice I made in the past, am I prepared to take steps to make a change right now? Otherwise I need to let

it go. But if I am willing to make change, then I need to take those steps.

INTERROGATING A THOUGHT: EXAMPLE

As an example, I will show you how I might break down a negative self talk thought with these questions:

Negative self talk: *I am a failure because I am single.*

- Who is this important to? *Being single is important to me. I'd like to share my life with someone. But it seems more important to my parents, who want me to be married like my brother and sister. Maybe it is more important to them, actually.*
- How much does this matter in the long run? *I want to eventually get married, so it matters in the long run. But I guess in "the long run" I have more time to find a partner.*
- Is my response an overreaction? *I have other areas of my life I feel successful in. My career is going well.*
- Am I overgeneralizing? Does my thought apply to everyone who is similar in this way to me? *Is everyone who is single a failure? No, there are a lot of people who choose to be single or are happy being single.*
- What is the concrete evidence for this thought? *I feel bad when I go to family gatherings without a partner. But those are my feelings. My parents always ask when I'm getting married. So their question is evidence that they think I'm a failure. No, it is concrete evidence that they want me to have a partner.*
- Am I viewing things in terms of absolutes? (Remember the "polarizing" type of negative self talk from the first chapter.) *Yes. I am defining myself as a failure because I am single.*
- Should it be more of a gray area? *Yes. I am not an absolute failure in every area of life, I guess.*
- Am I assuming the thoughts or feelings of others? *I am assuming that my parents think I'm a failure because they allude to wanting me to have a partner.*
- Am I using cruel language? *Failure is pretty harsh.*
- If I were having a positive thought about this, how would I interpret things? *I have a lot of time to pursue my own interests being single,*

30

and maybe I am doing so well at work because I don't have to worry about making extra time for a partner right now.

- What is the worst thing that could result from this? How likely is that to actually happen? If it did happen, what would be the next step I would take? *The worst thing that could happen is that I stay single forever. It could happen but it seems everyone finds someone at some point, so there is a chance I will find a partner. If I did end up single forever, the next step I would take is maybe adopting a child on my own.*

- Could the situation or feeling be worse? *Yes. I could be "older" with "less time" to find a partner. My grandma even found a new boyfriend at the nursing home a few years after my grandpa died. I have had dating experience before, it would be harder to date without my previous experience. I could live in a small town, instead of this big city, where there are more opportunities for dating.*

- Is this thinking going to help me achieve my goals? *Thinking I am a failure probably won't attract a partner.*

- What would help me feel better or think a different way? *I could try to not feel so ashamed about being single. Maybe then I'd put myself out there more for dating.*

- What can I learn from this thought? *I can learn that being single is a sore spot for me and something I'm sensitive about. Probably because my parents put pressure on me.*

- What is another way to interpret the situation? What would that mean? *Maybe I am less of a "failure" than my friends who got married too young and are already divorced. Though it's not nice to think of my friends as failures. That means if it's not nice to call them failures, it's not nice to call myself a failure.*

- What physical evidence for this exists, and how much is my feeling or perception? *I can't think of any physical evidence. I don't have a ring on my finger? That seems like a silly reason to be a failure, not wearing a piece of jewelry on a certain finger.*

- What is the evidence for my conclusion? *I guess there is no evidence, I just don't like going to events with friends where I know everyone will be a couple except me.*

- How would a friend talk to me about this thought? *A friend would probably tell me I need to date more and am not putting myself out there enough if I am not happy being single.*

- How would someone from a different culture or upbringing feel about this thought? *I guess some people have arranged marriages in other cultures and would probably want to be single like me.*

- If I am ruminating on a choice I made in the past, am I prepared to take steps to make a change right now? Otherwise I need to let it go. But if I am willing to make change, then I need to take those steps. *I sometimes wish I hadn't broken up with my boyfriend and imagine what our life would be like still together. But I don't want to get back with him, as our relationship was not good. So, no, I am not willing to make a change, so I should stop wasting time daydreaming about not having broken up with him. I should focus on the future instead.*

That is just one example of a way to interrogate a thought. The questions are very open-ended, so whatever direction your answers take you is fine. Just try to be as honest with yourself as possible and not let the negative thought win. Negative thoughts can be very powerful, and you may have to play a bit of "bad cop" with them, treating them as if they were hostile witnesses. Of course, that's just a fun metaphor, and you shouldn't be extremely critical of your own thoughts, as that is only furthering your negativity. We will talk about that in a later chapter, but for now, just try to assess your thoughts honestly and without judgment. In the next chapter, we'll look at the "Opposite Thought" strategy for turning around our self talk.

EXERCISE

For the exercise for this chapter, choose a thought and interrogate it using some or all of the questions found in this chapter. Your answers do not need to be long, but you can go as in-depth as you want. You may discover something revealing about where your negative thoughts are coming from or how they are holding you back, but also don't spend hours and hours on this task for a single thought, as that could be seen as rumination. Spend maybe 20 minutes on average to go through the list. You also don't need to write your answers down, but can just do them in your head. This will be good practice for positive and realistic self talk, too.

CHAPTER EIGHT

The Opposite Thought

Now that you know how to interrogate your negative self talk, we will move on to how you can reshape that negative talk into something more positive. The strategies in this chapter will revolve around an old tactic we all remember from childhood: The Opposite Game.

THINKING OPPOSITES

When we have negative self talk, one of the easiest strategies to use to try to flip our thoughts around is to think: *What is the opposite of what I've just thought about myself or this situation?*

For example, if you think, "Today is a crappy day because I forgot to send an important email this morning," just play a game with yourself where you think of the opposite thought. What would the opposite of this thought be? There is not one correct "opposite" answer, like "black is the opposite of white." The possibilities for opposite thoughts are infinite. Let's find a few based around the idea of why today is the opposite of a "crappy day:" Why it is a "great day."

- Today is a great day because I have a job
- Today is a great day because I have learned a valuable lesson about setting reminders for my most important tasks
- Today is a great day because I had a nice lunch with a new coworker
- Today is a great day because I am alive

You can make it as small as a good sandwich or as large as appreciating that you get to be alive. As long as the opposite thought is positive or realistic, it is the opposite of your negative thought.

Let's try another one: "I don't like my body." Just challenge yourself and your original position you are coming from. Each time you challenge yourself, you are making that new pathway through the forest, or building the new habits and thought patterns in your mind.

So if you are unhappy with your body, what are some amazing things your body allows you to do?

- Your eyes allow you to see a beautiful sunset.
- Your feet allow you to walk down the street.
- Your brain allows you to read or watch TV, activities you find pleasurable.
- Your nerves and skin allow you to feel the touch of another person, whether it is romantic or just a hug from a friend
- Your ears allow you to hear a song you like

So remember, the opposite strategy is as simple as asking yourself, what's the opposite of that thought I just had? It could be the key to reevaluating your approach to the world and your life. You can be as creative as you like.

RECOGNIZE YOUR STRENGTHS

When thinking of opposite thoughts, it is often important to recognize our own strengths. Of course, your strengths should actually be your strengths. They should be grounded in reality. Even if you feel down on yourself, we all have unique or good things about us that we can think about during a low point.

In the exercise for this chapter, you will write a list of your strengths.

It is also important to remember that even if something feels like a weakness for you, it is probably not as bad as you think.

For example, let's say you feel nervous about meeting new people, and you feel like you always make a poor first impression.

You may think, "I am not good at meeting new people."

(If this sounds like you, you may also enjoy my book on improving your social skills called "Small Talk: How to Talk to People, Improve Your Charisma, Social Skills, Conversation Starters & Lessen Social Anxiety.")

While this may feel true, you can think of a more positive thought, one that is more "growth mindset" rather than "fixed mindset." We are all always changing, and we do not have to be stuck as defined as one thing for our whole lives.

So, the opposite thought of "I am not good at meeting new people" wouldn't be "I am great at meeting new people," as it's probably not true for you. But you can think:

- "I am working on improving my social skills."
- "I am proud of myself for getting out of my comfort zone to meet new people, when it is an activity I recognize makes me nervous."
- "I am grateful I only feel that my skills could improve for meeting new people, and that I don't have a fear of leaving my house or diagnosed anxiety, which I imagine would be worse."

WATCH YOUR LANGUAGE

When constructing your opposite statements, it is helpful to avoid absolute statements.

Avoid words like "always" or "never." You don't have to be 100% or 0%, and in fact, nothing in life is that way. (Well, almost nothing.) If you don't get to the gym one day, you may think "I always screw up my workout routine," and then write off the whole week. Instead, just think, "I made a mistake here, and I am learning from this mistake and others I've made in the past." Don't forget to also look at the days you did make it to the gym. Let's say you want to get to the gym 3 days per week. If you miss 1 day, and only go 2 days out of the week, you may only ruminate on the 1 day you missed. But try to focus on wins, as well: "I made it to the gym 2 days this week. That's 2 more days that I would have gone 4 months ago, before I started being more conscious of my health." That's a huge win!

Don't get complacent, remember to learn from why you didn't hit your goal, but don't forget to focus on the positives.

You can also pay attention to the language you use to see whether it is neutral or judgmental. You can replace very negative statements that have cruel, judgmental language with more neutral language.

"I am fat," becomes "My body is bigger than I'd like it to be."

"I am a lazy worker," becomes "I could improve my focus at work."

"I feel stupid in meetings with my boss," becomes, "I feel unprepared for my meetings with my boss."

Do you see the difference? Take out judgmental, mean words like "fat," "lazy" and "stupid," from the way you talk to yourself, and replace them with less cruel words to describe yourself to yourself in your self talk.

These small changes in language seem like minor details, but the difference they can make is huge.

In the next chapter, we will look at gaining perspective when we have overwhelmingly negative self talk.

EXERCISE

In the exercise for this chapter, write down a list of your strengths. If you are feeling down on yourself, even coming up with one strength to focus on can make you feel a lot better. If you are having trouble coming up with your strengths, ask a friend or family member for help. Other people are often better at being positive about us than we are ourselves.

CHAPTER NINE

Perspective

We've already practiced taking a step back from thoughts and dis-identifying with them. Now we will practice taking a step back even from ourselves, to focus on others and get some perspective about our place in the world.

THINK ABOUT OTHERS

When you are suffering from negative self talk, it can feel like your problems are huge, as big as elephants stampeding through your living room, destroying everything in sight. How will you pick up all the pieces and carry on?

You can feel heavy, or like you are carrying a lot with you, like the saying "carrying the weight of the world on his shoulders." But one tactic you can use to ease this weight is to think about that world you feel like you are carrying.

You can focus your energy on others. This strategy can be helpful when you're throwing yourself a pity party. Everyone likes a pity party, when it's thrown just for one. But if you were to invite everyone in your social circles, it might quickly turn uncomfortable. You wouldn't want those people feeling bad for you, right? They probably all feel bad at some time or another, and they know what this feeling is like. Everyone has some negative thought patterns. Thinking about the lives and concerns of others can make us feel not so alone, and feel better, comparatively, to the problems of others. It's not about comparison, though. It's just about getting a quick dose of perspective when feeling down.

If you are feeling bad about your position in your company, for example, you may be comparing yourself to a friend with a seemingly impressive job title and high-powered career. But what if you know of another friend who is stressed about losing his or her job? You cannot always compare yourself to others you feel are doing better than you. To make this fair and realistic, you should also spend equal time thinking about people who are worse-off than you. Even if you don't feel you have an impressive job title, at least you are not worried about losing your job.

It is also important to recognize that suffering is a part of life. It is common to all of humanity, and you are not alone in your feelings and self-criticism. However, though everyone struggles, we all could do to struggle a little less. We have enough outside obstacles to overcome; why give ourselves more grief by adding to them with negative self talk? As you are learning in this book, changing your approach to the thoughts you tell yourself can ease that common suffering of humanity a little bit.

Laugh at Yourself

Another way to gain some perspective about the negative self talk you have about yourself and your life is to remember that life can be pretty absurd. Humor is a good antidote.

What feels a bit silly or funny to one person will not always resonate with someone else's funny bone, but whatever helps you cope and get some levity and distance from swirling negative thoughts can be yours to enjoy.

For example, if you're feeling a bit self-conscious at the gym, and it makes it hard for you to show up and get your butt off the couch, you can try to think about how absurd the idea of a gym is. Humans evolved fighting for survival in the African plains. Way back when, people didn't eat for days at a time, had to hunt, and struggled to put enough calories in their body that they would expend on a taxing hunt, often while going hungry. Today, humans are pretty comfortable, comparably. So comfortable, in fact, that we build big boxes with machines of varying movements just to exercise our rested bodies. What would cave people think of the muscled and toned people who spend so much time at the gym to make their body look a certain way? It's a bit absurd if you take a step back from it. That can give you just a little boost of confidence and a "who cares" attitude to get to the gym and not feel so intimidated.

It is worth mentioning again that all the strategies in this book are meant to help you, but you can cherry-pick which ones work for you and which ones don't.

People are Self-Focused

The last tactic to help you gain some perspective over your negative self talk is to ask yourself: Who cares?

Often, it is only you, and the extremely high standards you set for yourself. When we set ourselves up to fail, negative self talk can run rampant. Give your inner critic a day off sometimes. If you don't care, does anyone? (Of course, don't take this to the extreme of not caring about anything in your life. But it is OK to relax a bit sometimes instead of always being so negative and harsh on yourself. You may even find that being a bit kinder to yourself does wonders to your performance in areas you want to improve. But that is what we will get to in another chapter.)

When you think about "Who cares?" you can also remember that everyone is more focused on themselves than they are on anyone else. Aren't you reading a book about the way you talk to yourself inside your head? That we all have these constant thoughts should tell you a lot about how self-focused people are.

If you are having negative self thoughts about an impression you made or something embarrassing you feel you've done, the people you felt embarrassed in font of probably don't remember it as well as you do, or weren't thinking about you, but were in fact thinking about themselves.

Remembering that people are often worrying about themselves can take some of the pressure off of you.

In the next chapter, we will look at a few different ways to talk to yourself with different labels or names.

Exercise

For this exercise, choose either the strategy of thinking of others or the strategy of humor for one of your self talk thoughts. Assess the thought by thinking of others, or by taking a step back and enjoying the absurdity of life.

CHAPTER TEN

Naming

In this chapter we will look at a few different names you can use to turn around your negative self talk, names for either yourself or your inner critic.

TALK TO YOURSELF IN THE THIRD PERSON

One helpful way to change your negative self talk is to talk to yourself in the third person. This lets you be more objective. We are often better at seeing our friends' problems more clearly than our own, and better at giving advice to friends than to ourselves. If you say "you" instead of "I" when you talk to yourself in your head, you can be a bit more objective.

For example:
- "I am feeling nervous about my date tonight," becomes "You are feeling nervous about your date tonight."
- "I don't like my new haircut" becomes "You don't like your new haircut."

And so on and so-forth. It sounds a bit silly, but really, try it! It helps massively to make you gain a bit of space from your thoughts and realize how ridiculously negative some of them are.

It is also easier, when you talk to yourself as "you" instead of "I," to give yourself advice about how to feel better.

For example:
- "You will impress the boss at your work meeting today."
- "You will be able to socialize easily at the party tonight."

If you are finding the strategy of using "you" helps your internal monologue become much friendlier, you can take it one step further and talk to yourself by a nickname, or by your first name.

You can address yourself, like I would, with your name, like: "Aston, you are a good person." Or, you can use an endearing nickname, like, "Sweetie, don't beat yourself up about the cake you baked not being good."

This mental trick can help you get distance from yourself and feel a bit more positive and grounded. Even though it sounds silly, it really does work.

Name Your Inner Critic or Thoughts

Another tactic using naming is to name your inner critic, instead of naming yourself.

That voice in your head that is super mean and negative can feel a bit less daunting and scary with a name like "Bozo" or "Ebert the Self Critic." It also helps you to realize, once again, that you are not your thoughts. They can be put in this category of negative self talk, whatever you want to call it.

If you have a familiar thought pattern about one subject, you can give that a title as well. It is like giving a movie title, or a short story title, or maybe even a headline. Such as:

- "The My Friends are Cooler Than Me Radio Hour," when you have the same negative self talk about feeling like you don't fit in.
- "Revenge of the Small Work Mistake Part III," when you keep ruminating over something that happened last week and you can't change now.
- "Girl Jumps to Conclusions Again" as a headline when you start assuming what other people think of you without evidence.

You can use these naming strategies to help you be more aware of the negative self talk you experience. In the next chapter, we will look at self compassion as a strategy for addressing our self talk and using it in our favor instead of letting it work against us.

EXERCISE

For the exercise for this chapter, even if it feels a bit weird, write down some positive self talk using your own name, the word "you" or a nickname you have come up with for yourself.

CHAPTER ELEVEN

Self-Compassion

In this chapter we will look at self-compassion as a strategy for easing the strain we put on ourselves with negative self talk. Having more compassion for yourself can lead to more positive self talk.

WHAT IS SELF-COMPASSION?

Self-compassion is basically being kind to yourself, as you would have compassion or kindness for a stranger or a friend. We are often our own worst critics, and we are unreasonably harsh on ourselves, having higher standards for ourselves than others, and focusing more on the bad in our lives than we would were we counseling a friend.

When you practice self-kindness, you treat yourself as a friend. And shouldn't we all be our own friends? If you are not going to take responsibility for having some kindness for yourself, who will? You cannot count on others to always treat you fairly, but you can always treat yourself fairly.

Kindness is one of the most powerful things we have in human society and the capacity to feel as people. Everyone struggles, and being kinder than necessary on a daily basis is a good rule of thumb to follow, both for yourself and toward others.

As the author Kurt Vonnegut said in one of his books, "Hello, babies. Welcome to Earth. It's hot in the summer and cold in the winter. It's round and wet and crowded. At the outside, babies, you've got about a hundred years here. There's only one rule that I know of, babies—God damn it, you've got to be kind."

Part of being kind to yourself is accepting that you are human and you have flaws. We all have flaws. For some reason, we just don't allow ourselves to have them, only others. We do not need to embrace our flaws and love them. Life should always be about improving yourself and your actions, I believe. But being kind to yourself does mean forgiving yourself for your flaws while working to improve them.

WHY YOU SHOULD BE KIND TO YOURSELF

Why should you be compassionate toward yourself? Studies show that self-compassion can be even more important in successful people than high self-esteem. This can feel counterintuitive: Being kind to yourself about your weaknesses is more important than feeling super confident about your strengths.

So if you actively work to turn your negative self talk into kinder self talk, this is even more important than running endless pump-up motivational "You can do it!" mantras in your head. This is why assessing our negative self talk is so essential to living a better life.

Having compassion for yourself has been shown to be stronger in people who are going through tough times and prevailing. They often have higher adaptability, or resiliency, to be able to bounce back from these trials than those who do not feel compassion for themselves.

So having nicer inner self talk is important to being more prepared for whatever you go through in life.

SELF-COMPASSION TECHNIQUES

One tactic for self compassion that you have probably heard of is positive affirmations. In popular culture, these are done in front of a mirror, but you can choose to practice them in your head while on your commute, walking the dog, getting ready for work, or if you like, in front of the mirror.

Positive affirmations are things like:
- "I am beautiful."

- "I am worthy."
- "I am a good person."

You should be cautious with positive affirmations, however. Some self-help gurus advise you put your goals into positive affirmations. So if your goal is to be a millionaire, but right now you are not, they would advise you use the positive affirmation of "I am a millionaire." However, studies show that false affirmations that are not true can make a person feel worse, not better, in their self talk. Positive affirmations should be things that you know to be true, but that you have a hard time telling yourself. You are beautiful, but it can be difficult for you to believe it. This could be an effective positive affirmation. I do not recommend, however, using affirmations that are aspirational, goals, or not yet true.

Another form positive affirmations can take instead of "I am" statements is the less forceful "May I" statements, such as:

- "May I feel beautiful today."
- "May I feel worthy today."
- "May I forgive myself."
- "May I be kind to myself today."
- "May I be patient."

These "May I" statements are almost a question or a wish. They give you permission to feel beautiful today, instead of the "I am beautiful" that can be a bit more difficult to adopt into your life. Choose whichever tactic makes more sense or feels more right to you.

A second tactic for self-compassion is to imagine what a friend would say to you, or imagine what you would say to a friend who had your problem. It is easier to be compassionate to others than it is to ourselves, so use this mental trick to think what a friend would say to you if they heard the way you talk to yourself. If you're having a mean thought about yourself that you wouldn't say to a friend, then why would you be cruel enough to say it to yourself?

One last tactic for self-compassion is compassionate self-touch. We feel better when we get a hug from someone who cares about us when we are feeling down, or maybe when someone rests a caring hand on our arm. In the absence of a close friend, we can do these things for ourselves. While it sounds silly, the body responds to touch and warmth, even if it is our own. You can lay your hand over your heart, rest your hand on your arm or stroke your arm, or cradle your face in your hands. The body will respond, and the mind will follow. Just opening yourself up to this compassionate self-touch may make you more open to compassionate self-talk.

Exercise

The exercise for this chapter is the following writing exercise: Choose something you are insecure about or that makes you feel "not good enough." Write down all the feelings you have surrounding that idea, and maybe even the self talk you say to yourself about it. Then pretend the concerns you have written down are those of a friend. Choose a friend you know well, and address them by name to really imagine that the problem is theirs What advice would you give to a friend with this problem? How would you remind them of their humanity, and that we are all human and have flaws and good traits? Don't read the letter now, or immediately after you are done writing it. Leave this letter for a week or more, and then open it up again, and you will be able to read it with fresh eyes, and you will see that you possess great compassion and wisdom for others. If you can direct it at a friend, you can direct it at yourself.

CHAPTER TWELVE

Constructive Negative Self Talk

"Positive thinking" has exploded in recent years as a world-wide phenomenon. But in this book, we aim for something more like "constructive thinking," "realistic thinking," or "optimistic thinking" vs. an overwhelming positive approach to everything. You'll see why.

COMPASSION TOWARD NEGATIVE THOUGHTS

The first thing about constructive self talk to note is that we should not hate our negative thoughts or our inner critic. While they can be quite cruel and difficult to be rid of once they are ingrained in our thought patterns, feeling negatively toward them or hating them only brings more negativity and cruelty into your state of mind.

Instead, feel a bit of compassion for your negative thoughts. Imagine that they have good intentions. After all, we all want to be better. Reciting our perceived flaws to ourselves over and over is quite an ineffective method of getting rid of the flaws we feel so badly about, but sometimes, that's what our brain is attempting to do.

So, we can thank our brain for trying to help us become better. We don't have to like the negative thoughts, but we shouldn't direct our anger at them.

Without any negative thoughts, we'd be perfectly complacent satisfying our immediate needs all the time, instead of planning for long-term goals, improving the way we approach our life and relationships, basically everything.

Be kind to your negative thoughts as you bid them farewell from your brain, and we take a look at the ways to turn those negative thought patterns into more constructive thought patterns.

Realistic Thinking & Positive Thinking

You may have heard of "positive thinking" before. Positive thinking has become quite an extreme self-help idea, and it is not one I suggest the readers of this book subscribe to. Many theories of positive thinking want you to approach everything in life with an unending sunniness. Whether you lose your job, grieve the death of a loved one, fall ill, or experience whatever difficulty that is affecting your life, the theory of positive thinking wants you to think happy thoughts about it.

I believe that this approach to life can actually make you worse off than feeling difficult emotions. That could be a topic for a whole new book.

For the purposes of self talk, I want to clearly state that this book is not about turning any negative thought you have into a 100% happy thought. The purpose of this book is to help you become aware of the subconscious patterns of thought you are running in your mind, and how those thoughts, when overwhelmingly negative instead of based in reality or being constructive, keep you from leading a happier life and achieving your goals.

So our goal will not be to turn all of your thoughts into positive thinking. Our goal will be to turn your negative thoughts into either constructive negative thoughts, neutral and nonjudgmental thoughts, or, if appropriate, positive thoughts.

Let's look at how we can turn our negative thoughts into constructive thoughts that work for us instead of against us.

Constructive Criticism

An easy solution to negative self talk would be the method of positive thinking. If we could simply dismiss all of our negative feelings about ourselves, it would be as simple as that. What we want to do instead of turning negative thinking into positive thinking is to turn negative thinking into more constructive thinking, so that we can help ourselves improve in areas that feel we need to. Of course, negative thoughts can be quite extreme, and we shouldn't believe them 100%, just like we shouldn't dismiss them 100%. What we can do instead is make them kinder, more positive, and more constructive.

When you have a lot of negative self talk that is harmful, your inner critic is like a movie critic. They just watch what's happening in your life and they criticize what they like or don't like, without becoming involved. What your inner critic needs to be is a combination of an inner coach and an inner friend. If your negative self talk is around your exercise regimen, your inner critic is like a drill instructor, berating you, yelling at you, and making you feel terrible. What if your inner critic could instead be like a workout buddy? An accountability partner? A friend who is encouraging, but also a little tough-love when she tells you that you have to get to the gym today with her, no matter your excuses?

These are some helpful metaphors for a way to think about the way you talk to yourself. You can adopt strategies from previous chapters that fit into this idea, like using an endearing nickname for yourself, talking to yourself in the third person, gaining humor or perspective, and getting distance from your negative thoughts.

Building up an inner constructive monologue vs. destructive monologue is about encouraging yourself, not being overly harsh, being more positive, and acknowledging your flaws while not blowing them out of proportion.

Here are some examples of negative self talk becoming constructive self talk:

- "I am so ugly" becomes "What about my appearance do I have control over that I can work to change?"
- "I am not good at social interactions" becomes "I can get better at social interactions through practice."
- "I get stressed too easily" becomes "I am feeling stressed right now, but it is just a feeling."

In the next chapter, we will look at a few external factors you may want to consider during your journey toward healthier self talk.

EXERCISE

For the exercise for this chapter, pick a topic that you have negative self talk about. Write down your thoughts from the perspective of the cruel, negative self talk critic, like the movie critic or drill sergeant. Now write down inner chatter from the perspective of an encouraging friend with a little dose of tough love.

CHAPTER THIRTEEN

Outside Influences to Consider

Though we have, in previous chapters, looked at how changing our external circumstances won't change our internal dialogue with ourselves, there are three areas of your life that I believe will help you considerably in your journey towards a healthier life and healthier self talk. We will look at meditation, health and friends.

MEDITATION

Meditation and mindfulness, as I will use them here, are interchangeable terms. You may have heard of one or both of them before. While meditation has been around for thousands of years, mindfulness has only entered the popular lexicon recently.

Both traditions mean having more awareness of your body, your mind and your thoughts. If you want to take up a formal meditation practice, you can start by sitting quietly and trying to notice your thoughts and not becoming attached to them for just 5 or 10 minutes a day. There are a number of beginner apps out there for your phone if you think this will be helpful to you.

You can also start practicing more meditation and mindfulness by focusing on your breath when you are in a stressful situation or feeling extremely emotional. Taking just 5 deep breaths will give you the space you need, will help calm down your nervous system, and will give you a break before you react emotionally and quickly to something.

Another technique is to just take a break to notice your surroundings or your thoughts when going about your day. Whether you are walking to work, driving, sitting at your computer, eating a meal, or talking to a friend, focus on what you can see, hear, smell, touch or taste. How do your hands feel on the steering wheel? What is your friend saying? Listen intently. How does each individual flavor taste? How do they work together? Being more present in the immediate moment can also help you to feel calmer and more aware of your thoughts and experiences.

Overall, just taking pause throughout your day can greatly improve your own mental chatter. I think you will find that some mindfulness in your life will help you greatly reroute the patterns of self talk you have built in your mind.

DIET & EXERCISE

Another factor that I believe can have a big impact on changing your inner self talk is taking care of your body. While many people find they have a lot of negative self talk around these very topics, working towards them can give you a big leg up in rerouting your brain patterns.

The idea behind the mind-body connection is that the health of our minds and our bodies is closely linked. By putting healthy food into your body and moving it around with at least some light exercise a few days a week, you keep your brain in the best health possible as well. Start with small goals, like just putting on your gym shoes to go get the mail. You may find you end up walking around the block. Or just choosing the side salad instead of a side of fries with a juicy burger.

Taking care of our bodies goes a long way toward taking care of our mental health.

SOCIAL CIRCLE

The last external factor that I think makes a big difference toward our inner monologues is surrounding ourselves with people who also have healthy and more positive-leaning thought patterns. There is a saying that you are the average of the 5 people you spend the most time with. Being around positive people will naturally make you more positive. When you talk to yourself negatively less often, and become more aware of it, you will probably become more aware of how the people around you talk negatively. You may find that you naturally don't enjoy being around people you didn't notice were so negative before.

Meditation, health and social circles are three external factors that can help you make the thought patterns in your brain healthier, more positive and more constructive.

EXERCISE: EXERCISE!

For this chapter's exercise, take one step toward bettering one area from this chapter. Call a positive friend to grab coffee and catch up. Meditate for 10 minutes. Go for a walk, or to the gym, or eat vegetables with dinner tonight. Make one small change that you can claim as a "win" in the area of meditation, health or social circles.

CONCLUSION

Thank you for reading "Self Talk," and I hope you have learned something from this short book. The relationship we have with ourselves is the longest and most guaranteed one we will experience our entire lives. We can never escape ourselves, so we might as well make ourselves into our best friends and biggest supporters. I truly believe that begins with positive self talk. Too many people are too harsh on themselves, and I think we could all benefit from more kindness and positivity in our lives toward ourselves.

If you have followed along in these chapters and performed the exercises, you are well on your way to a healthier inner life. Changing your self talk isn't easy, and can be a life-long journey. Continue to reference this book for strategies to help you with your own inner self talk, and go slow as you build new, happier thoughts and habits.

If you enjoyed this book, I'd really appreciate you leaving me a review. Getting feedback from real readers like yourself is what helps me improve my books and keep writing more.

Leave a review on the book's Amazon page by typing this link into your browser: bit.ly/selftalkreview

FURTHER READING

If you enjoyed this book by author Aston Sanderson, please check out the book "Small Talk: How to Talk to People, Improve Your Charisma, Social Skills, Conversation Starters & Lessen Social Anxiety."

You can buy it here: http://bit.ly/smalltalkbook

Subscribe to the Free Book Club at **www.walnutpub.com** for more books from author Aston Sanderson, and free new releases from Walnut Publishing.

Thanks for reading!

Made in the USA
Middletown, DE
21 January 2018